Annamaria Giusti

ARLES

97 Photographs in colour

BONECHI

© Copyright 1981 by
CASA EDITRICE BONECHI
Via dei Cairoli 18/b - Firenze
Telex 571323 CEB

ISBN 88-7009-169-4

Photographic service by
LUIGI DI GIOVINE

Translated by
JOHN SWEET

Diffusion:
VETS - Villeneuve-lès-Avignon
Tél. (90) 252863

Arles seen from the river Rhone.

HISTORICAL OUTLINE

The appearance of the region around Arles was very different in prehistoric times than it is today: the sea made a deep estuary, later filled by the alluvial deposits brought down by the Rhone, so creating huge marshes dotted with rocky islets which were inhabited by a primitive population of ligurians. The ancient Celtic name for Arles was "Arlaith", trasformed by the Romans into "Arelate", which probably means "the place of the marsh".

Around 1100 B.C. Phoenician merchants began to visit this region bringing with them the first movement towards civilization, this was continued by the Greeks four centuries later who established their colonies here, including Arles which was founded by the Greeks of Marseilles in a convenient location for maritime and river commerce. The effects of Greek civilization on Arles were not erazed by the arrival of the Celts, a barbarian tribe who established themselves here and gradually throughout the area of Provence, but continued to flourish and influenced the following Roman period which began at Arles in 49 B.C.. In that year Caesar, having conquered Pompey, wished to repay the naval help he had received from the Gallic city and founded a colony for his veterans here with the title "Colonia Iulia Paterna Arelatensis Sextanorum", bestowing

3

on it all the privileges reserved for the colonies directly founded by him. Arles now began a period of growth that was to continue until the end of the Roman Empire, it was favoured by a strategic position on the Rhone delta, along land communications routes, and was also surrounded by a fertile region guaranteeing it a rich agricultural production. Octavian Augustus and after him all the Roman Emperors always treated this smiling city, which was an important centre for the economy and trade of a vast empire, with a special benevolence. In importance and vitality Arles emerged with the other centres of Gallia Narbonese and was gradually enriched with important public works which could compete with any of the major cities of the Roman world: the theatre, the amphitheatre, an acqueduct 75 kilometres long, baths, warehouses for merchantise and also streets, squares, fountains, elegant villas decorated with mosaic and sculpture mainly produced by the busy workshops of the local artists.

Already by the 1st century B.C. Provence was rapidly being converted to Christianity and it is significant that Arles itself was chosen in 314 as the meeting place for the first great council of the Christian Church; during these years, thanks to the favour of the Emperor Constantine, the city experienced a particularly prosperous period, acquiring the appearance and the importance of a capital, a title wich was officially bestowed in 418 in an edict of Emperor Honorious. But by now the Roman Empire was coming to an end, and Provence was one of the border territories most exposed to barbarian incursions. From 426 onwards Arles was subject to several Visigothic attacks until finally it succumbed definitively in 480.

The most disasterous period for the city now begins, it lost its ancient splendour and was fought over by the Visigoths, the Franks, the Ostrogoths and even suffered Saracen invasions. From the 9th century Arles became the capital of a kingdom that included part of Provence and the Bourgogne and though caught up in stormy political and military events a period of economic and artistic revival began for the city that reached its peak between the 12th and 13th centuries. The last king of Provence was René d'Anjou whose family, the Earls of Provence, had provided stable government for the kingdom for over two centuries, since 1239, making it a centre of culture, of art and a refined way of life. In 1423 Provence, and with it Arles, was absorbed into the kingdom of France and from then on shared its fate. For Arles this meant an elegant but inevitable decline which made it play a secondary role to Aix and Marseilles, though river and sea commerce retained a certain prosperity. The arrival of the railways in 1884 reduced enormously the importance of the Rhone as a commercial and communications route and since then the economy of the city and the surrounding area acquired and maintains a mainly agricultural appearance. Arles has escaped from the ravages of time and of those more recent ones often brought on industrial civilization, in its ancient stones and monuments Arles keeps alive the fascination and the memory of a noble past.

Place de la République with the Egyptian obelisk and the church of St. Trophime. ▶

SAINT TROPHIME

The Romanesque artistic achievement left many famous works in Provence, among the most remarkable of these monuments is the Cathedral of St. Trophime.

St. Trophime was chosen by the citizen of Arles as their patron saint from the earliest centuries of Christianity. According to an old tradition he had been sent from Greece by St. Peter himself; he evangelized the whole of this area and converted the Gallic tribes. The founding of the first basilica is attributed to him, it was dedicated to St. Stephen whose head St. Trophime had brought from Judea.

A Saracen raid in the early 8th century destroyed this first basilica; reconstruction begun during the Carolingian period but the important architectural modifications were undertaken during the 12th century when the façade and the cloisters received their rich, sculptural decoration. On the 29th September the reliques of St. Trophime were solemnly translated here from their original resting place in the suburban cemetery of Les Alyscamps. The renovated church was dedicated to him and has since become a cathedral. Emperor Frederick Barberossa received the royal crown of Provence here on the 30th July 1178 from the hands of Archbishop Raymond de Bolène, and it was here that the last king of Provence, René d'Anjou, married Jeanne de Laval.

The magnificent portal, shaped like a triumphal arch supported by a row of small columns, stands out against the undeco-

St. Trophime: the façade.

St. Trophime: the portal in the form of an arch of triumph.

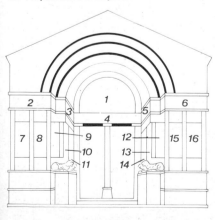

1 - Last Judgement: blessing Christ with the symbols of four Evangelists (the lion of St. Mark, the ox of St. Luke, the eagle of St. John and the angel of St. Matthew).
2 - The chosen go to Christ.
3 - The chosen are presented by an angel to Abraham, Isaac and Jacob.
4 - The twelve Apostles with the Gospel.
5 - The sinners turned out of the Paradise Gates by an angel.

6 - The damned are taken to the Hell by a demon.
7 - St. Bartholomew.
8 - St. James the Elder.
9 - St. Trophime.
10 - St. John the Evangelist.
11 - St. Peter with the keys.
12 - The martyrdom of St. Stephen.
13 - St. Andrew.
14 - St. Paul.
15 - St. James the Younger.
16 - St. Philip.

St. Trophime - Portal: lunette with the representation of Christ as Judge.

rated stone façade whose lower section is of Carolingian origin; it abounds with statues, relief figures and ornamental friezes. The influence of the art of Ancient Rome is obvious both in the architecture and in the sculptural decoration, in Provence this inheritance was never completely lost during the late Middle Ages and its essence survived to nourish the great flourishing of Romanesque in Provence. Both in the general lay out and in the location of specific scenes the portal of St. Trophime restates the slightly earlier portal of the Abbey of St. Gilles where the

sculpture shows the first energetic assertion of the Provencal School.

The reliefs of the *Last Judgement* occupy the architrave, the lunette and the entablature above the little columns in the portal of St. Trophime. Thi theme occurs frequently in the art of the Middle Ages, and particularly in French sculpture: central prominence is given to the dignified figure of *Christ as Judge*, within a mandorla, between the *symbols of the Four Evangelists.* Below, on the architrave, are *the Apostles and the Patriachs* while on the left a *Procession of the Elect* moves

towards Christ and to the right *the Damned* move away to enter the flames of Hell.

Between the columns are ten powerful *figures of saints*, they show the reacquisition of form in its dimensional and architectural aspects which characterizes Provencal Romanesque sculpture.

The **interior** of St. Trophime is divided into a nave and two aisles, a floor plan which is common among the Romanesque churches of Provence: the aisles are narrow and dark and have barrel vaults while in the central nave ogive vaulting already appears heralding the later developments of the Gothic. The church has many important works of sculpture of an even earlier period: on the left of the entrance the baptesimal font is built around the frontal piece of a Paleochristian sarcophagus; the altar of the 17th century chapel in the north transept rests on a sculpted sarcophagus depicting the *Crossing of the Red Sea* that probably dates from the end of the 4th century and shows qualities of expressive liveliness and formal elegance which characterizes the sculpture of this region during late Roman times. Another sarcophagus, from the middle of the 4th century, carved with a series of *Saints* is set within a double row of low arches; it retains, both in the figures and in the decoration, a tight bond with Paleochristian reliefs demostrating that the knowledge and imitation of ancient sculpture was never lost in the Provence throughout the Middle Ages.

St. Trophime - Portal: bas-reliefs representing the martyrdom of St. Stephen, St. James and St. Philip.

St. Trophime - Portale: bas-relief representing St. Bartholomew, St. James the Minor and St. Trophime.

◄ In the preceding pages: St. Trophime - Interior: sarcophagus representing the Crossing of the Red Sea and sarcophagus with figures of saints; the main altar within the church.

THE CLOISTER

The canons of the Cathedral originally led a communal monastic existence which explains the conventual buildings and **the cloisters** alongside St. Trophime; due to the abundance and the quality of the sculptural decoration this place has a very moving atmosphere. The north and east sections of the cloisters are the most ancient, they were built in Romanesque style in the 12th century with round arches and barrel vaulting while the south and the west sections date from the 14th century with loggias and ogival vaulting; on all four sides the capitals of the compound columns and the loggias and the solid corner pilasters are sculpted with *scenes from the Old and the New Testament* and with *the Life of St. Trophime and the Three Marys* who were particularly venerated during the Middle Ages in this part of Provence. The sculpture on the north side is the earliest (1150-60) shortly preceding that of the church's façade. These also draw directly from the sculptural style of St. Gilles but the vibrant animation is translated into more peaceful and contained forms which create in the plasticity of the statuary a sense of dignified and restrained strengt. The sculpture of the north side has similar subject matter and was carried out several decades later, though they are of excellent quality they still reveal a certain

A view of the cloister of St. Trophime, with the beautiful rectangular bell tower.

The garden in the cloister, seen from one of the galleries.

slackening of the expressive tension. The sculptural decoration on the corner pilasters of the cloister acquires a monumental dimension in the majestic triads of saints sculpted in high relief alternating with reliefs of biblical subjects. The influence of the great models of Roman sculpture are more clearly recognizable here than in the capitals, these gave the artists of St. Trophime the sense of mastery of the plastic form and the sense of rediscovering the dignity of the human condition. In one of the rooms of the monastery which open off the cloisters is a small **museum** where lovely Aubusson tapestries from the 17th century are displayed depicting *Scenes from the Life of the Virgin* and a contemporary series of Flemish tapestries with a *History of the Jews* which were once intended for the austere interior of St. Trophime.

13

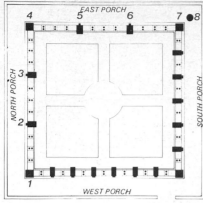

1 - St. Peter, St. Trophime and St. John the Evangelist.
2 - Resurrection of Christ among the pilgrims of Emmaus.
3 - Incredulity of St. Thomas and St. James.
4 - St. Paul, Ascension of Christ, St. Stephen, the martyrdom of St. Stephen and St. Andrew.
5 - Flagellation of Christ among his persecutors and Judas.
⌐ - The Lamb, symbol of Christ, between Solomon and the Queen of Sheba.
7 - Gamaliel, master of St. Paul; washing of the feet, the Supper and Judas kiss.
8 - The well.

◄ South-east corner of the cloister: the well whose arched lintel is formed on the base of an ancient theater column.

◄ North-west pilaster of the cloister, with the statues of St. Peter, St. Trophime (at center) and St. John.

Detail of the north-west pilaster with the portrayal of St. Trophime, first bishop of the city of Arles.

Detail of nort-west pilaster: at left St. Andrew, at center St. Stephen and at right St. Paul. The three saints frame reliefs portraying the martyrdom of St. Stephen and the Ascension.

East gallery: a capital with vegetal decoration and another with the representation of an eagle.

East gallery: a capital with vegetal decoration and another with a representation of the Annunciation.

1 - East gallery: capital with the Flight into Egypt and the angel's warning.

2 - East gallery: the apostles set out to preach the Evangel.

3 - East Gallery: the Nativity.

4 - East gallery: the Slaughter of the Innocents.

1

3

2

4

A view from above of the cloister of St. Trophime and the bell-tower.

Museum of the Cloister: overall view of the hall and (below) detail of an Aubusson tapestry with stories from the life of the Virgin.

Place de la République, with the Egyptian obelisk at center, the Church of St. Anne with its Museum of Pagan Art at left and the Town Hall in the background.

PLACE DE LA REPUBLIQUE

The Place de la Republique is the lively centre of the town surrounded by famous monuments which sum up the artistic history of the city: the Romanesque Cathedral of St. Trophime, the façade of the late Gothic Church of St. Anne and the classical mass of the 17th century Hôtel de Ville all face into it. The centre is dominated by the striking silhouette of the Egyptian obelisk which once stood in the Circus of ancient Roman Arles. The obelisk was transferred here from the centre of the "spina" - the circuit reserved for chariot races - in 1675, during the reign of Louis XIV and set up on a high pedistal decorated with lions and bronze masks, in the centre of a fountain.

HÔTEL DE VILLE

The bright classical prospect of the Hôtel de Ville, certainly the most interesting of the civil buildings in Arles, is framed by the severe façade of the Church of St. Anne and the impressive majesty of the portal of St. Trophime. The northern section and the sturdy bell tower survive from an earlier period. The latter was built in 1547 and crowned a few years later with *a bronze statue of the God Mars*; he is depicted as a daring warrior who, from above, watches over the city's fortunes in war, at that time Arles was involved in the struggle against Charles V who was attempting the conquest of Provence.

The enlargement of the Hôtel de Ville was undertaken in the 16th century from the project of Peytret with the final alterations by the famous architect Mansart who, with his ornate classicism, influenced much of the French architecture of the period. His style may be recognized here in the clear divisions of the façade stressed by Corinthian pilasters and decorated with sculpted heads and garlands, and also in the huge ground floor chamber supported by ten pairs of columns. A wide stairway leads from here to the upper floors where a copy of the famous Venus of Arles is placed, the original was discovered during excavations of the Roman Theatre in 1651 and is now in the Louvre.

The statue of the god Mars atop the tower of the Town Hall.

The ground floor of the Town Hall, with a copy of the Venus of Arles.

MUSEUM OF PAGAN ART

A valuable collection of lapidary works from Roman times is housed in the Church of St. Anne, built with a contribution from King Louis XIII during the first decades of the 17th century in a style that was still inspired by Gothic architectural models. The austere interior of the church has become an evocative setting for the series of sculpture and mosaics collected together here dating from the 1st to the 3rd centuries A.D., the period when Arles emerged as one of the most important and artistically creative centres of Gallia Narbonese.

One of the most remarkable pieces to point out is a powerful *statue of Medea* contemplating the murder of her sons, the body is full of impetus and the face of rage. This is recognizable as the work of a local artist who, though inspired by Hellenistic sculpture was able to supply an original, simplified and dramatic

Interior view of the Pagan Lapidary Museum.

Sarcophagus inspired by the myth of Phaedra and Hippolytus representing vivid scenes of hunting.

version. On the other hand the large mutilated *statue of Augustus* placed in the apse is characteristic of Classical calmness and gravity, it was found in the ancient Theatre of the city. However the most famous piece recovered during the excavations, the famous *Venus of Arles*, is not here; it was found amongst the ruins of the Theatre in 1651 and although it was broken in three places and the arms were damaged the statue was of such beauty that the people of Arles were convinved that they should present it to the Sun King. It was restored and completed by Girardon, the sculptor, and in this state the Venus is still kept in the collection of the Louvre. All that remains in Arles is a cast made by the sculptor Péru when the statue was found which shows its appearance before the alterations by Girardon.

Of the sarcophagi collected by the museum, the one depicting *the myth of Phaedrus and Hippolyte* is particularly interesting: it was found in the ancient quarter of Trinquetaille at the end of the last century. It shows lively hunting scenes worked with that acute realistic sense that characterizes Roman sculpture particular of the Provencal area. The floor mosaics with coloured tessera which once decorated the sumptous Gallo-Roman villas also came from Trinquetaille; between the refined geometric and decorative setting are representative scenes inspired by themes from Greek mythology; *the rape of Europa, Jason and the Golden Fleece, Orpheus* enchanting the wild beasts with his lyre.

Detail of a mosaic representing the Rape of Europa.

ORPHÉE

The myth of Orpheus depicted on a mosaic floor.

THEATRE

If the Amphitheatre is the most famous Roman building in Arles, the oldest is the Theatre; some say it was built around 30 B.C., and others from 20 to 15 B.C., in either case during the reign of Augustus. It stands in the eastern part of the city where the ground is slightly inclined, this was used to create the "cavea", able to hold 12,000 specatators on its steps.

As it originally appeared the Theatre of Arles must have been one of the most prestigious monuments of Gallia Narbonense, capable of withstanding comparison with the majestic buildings in the Rome of Augustus. It was surrounded by three orders of arcades and on the stage the grandiose portico was supported by slender Corinthian columns of which only two survive, for this reason they are popularly known as the "Deux Veuves", the two widows.

A gigantic statue of Augustus, three metres tall, dominated the stage, fragments of it still survive and are kept in the Museum of

The ruins of the Roman Theatre, with the two Corinthian columns called "deux veuves".

A view of the Theatre during a folklore performance.

Pagan Art. Alongside it stood a statue of Diana (only the head has been found) and a statue of Venus, uncovered on the 6th June 1651 and presentedi by the city to Louis XIV.

Although the Theatre, as we see today, lacks its rich sculptural decoration and also most of the architectural structure has been destroyed (from the 5th century Christian fanaticism systematically pillaged it, carrying away stone after stone to be used as construction material for churches, private dwellings and the wall fortifications), it remains a picturesque and vital setting for the shows and performances that are held here particularly during the month of July. It is then that Arles abandons its quiet and rather sleepy appearance and offers an extraordinary festival rich in artistic and cultural events of an excellent standard.

The Theatre is also the lovely setting for the celebrations of local traditions and folklore, such as the **Festival of the Queen of Arles** in which groups from all over Provence participate with songs and dances. The local costume of the Arlesienne stands out from

27

the others for its severe and highly refined elegance, it is gathered over the breast by a small, organza and lace shawl which brings to mind the soft grace and coquettishness of the late 18th century. The noble elegance of the dress is completed by the hair styling, the hair is lifted from the nape to form almost a natural diadem into which the girls fix an light knot of lace in the shape of butterfly wings and the married women a wide ribbon of coloured silk.

◀ *Vivaciuos Catalanian costumes worn for a popular festival in the Theatre.*

◀ *Popular dances in the Theatre.*

The typical "gardians" from the nearby Camargue region on their white horses.

Arlesian women dressed in their characteristic folk costume for the "Festival of the Queen of Arles".

Another scene of the popular dances near the ancients columns of the Theatre.

In this view from above, the Arena can be recognized with the ancient Theatre slightly below it.

ARENA

The most representative monument of ancient Roman Arles is the Amphitheatre, a mighty eliptical construction opened on the exterior by a double order of arcades, each made up of 60 arches, Doric above and Corinthian below, and divided internally by 43 rows of steps. It is the dimensions of the elipse that are most striking: 136 metres long by 107 wide.

The Amphitheatre was built at the time of the Emperor Hadrain to accomodate at least 25,000 seated spectators. Popular shows and entertainments were held there, combats between gladiators and wild beasts took place on the huge central oval which was surrounded by a high wall to protect the spectators from the attacks of the wild animals.

On the outer walls, which are built of huge stone blocks and originally had a third level of arcades, are raised three medieval towers. They are evidence of a time when the Amphitheatre was transformed into a kind of fortified stronghold bristling with little shops, stables, the houses of the poor of the city, and even two chapels were built there. Only in 1825 the Arles' local government ordered the Amphitheatre to be cleared, the later additions to be knocked down and the original architecture to be recovered.

The Arena has regained its function as a place for popular enter-

External view of the Arena.

The interior of the Arena.

The Rhone seen from the upper parapet of the Arena.

The outer wall and tower of the Arena.

A Spanish-style bullfight in the Arena.

tainments and today bull-fights like the Spanish ones take place there, often the bulls are from the nearby Camargue: small but full of fighting spirit. Less bloody entertainments are also held there, such as the traditional festival of the Guardians of the Camargue, or the "course à la cocade". This is a competition requiring courage and training which also has comic moments:

the competitors, on foot, called *razateurs*, must pierce a red cocarde fixed between the horns of a bull with a forked hook. The bull in this context is called a *cocardier* and the shouts and excitement of the crowd are for him; one of these animals, the famous Clairon even had a statue erected to him by the inhabitants of Beaucaire in a square of their city.

A scene from the bullfight.

The traditional "course à la cocarde", engaging men and Camarge bulls.

37

Sarcophagus representing Concordius, bishop of Arles, who died about 390. This sarcophagus was known as the "tomb of the moon" because the water which always filled it increased and diminuished in quantity as the moon waxed and waned. For this reason, miraculous beliefs grew up around it. At the center, the seated Christ is represented flanked by the Evangelists Matthew, Mark, Luke and John.

Overall view of the Chapel of the Jesuits, where the Museum is housed. ▶

MUSEUM OF CHRISTIAN ART

The bright interior of the old Jesuit church, built in the 17th century contains a valuable collection of Paleochristian sarcophagi from the 4th centuries, comparable in importance to that of the Vatican Museums in Rome. In style these densely carved sarcophagi continue the tradition of pagan sculpture which had been particularly lively and productive in Arles since the time of Augustus, but the subjects and the personages are new, often inspired by biblical or gospel texts.

Most of the pieces brought together here come from the cemetery of Les Alyscamps, situated on the outskirts of the city which, from the 4th century, was enriched by the statues and the sarcophagi of the Christians who were buried here. The indifference of the Middle Ages and the custom, established in the 16th century, of making gifts of the most beautiful pieces to powerful visitors led to the dispersion of many of the sculptural treasures of Les Alyscamps until, in the last century, it was decided to save the surviving works and bring them together in this museum. Almost to compensate for the devastation it suffered the soil of Arles continues still to throw up valuable evidence of its past, such as the three excellent sarcophagi on display here, discovered in 1974 at Trinquetaille, an ancient part of the city on the right bank of the river. In the museum is also the entrance to an imposing underground gallery shaped like a horse shoe, built in the 1st century B.C. to be used as a grain deposit.

"Sarcophagus of the Trinity", i[n]
marble, dating from the secon[d]
quarter of the fourth century.
On the cover, scenes from the
Old Testament: among them a[n]
extremely rare scene in the
iconography of Arles, that of
the creation of woman and her
presentation to Adam,
witnessed by the Holy Trinity.

"Sarcophagus of the Hunt",
from the second quarter of the
fourth century, also in marble.
The theme of the decoration is
of clearly pagan inspiration, sti[ll]
fashionable in the mid-fourth
century.

Sarcophagus in Carrara marble, dating from about the year 400 A.D., representing Christ consigning the Book of the Law to Peter. At the center, Christ at the summit of the mountain from which flow the four rivers of Paradise, is in the act of handing over the Law to Peter, who bears the cross. In the niche at far left, the washing of feet is represented; in the following niche, St. Paul holds the phoenix, symbol of Resurrection.

Detail of the sarcophagus representing the consignment of the law to Peter: Christ is brought before Pilate by two soldiers.

The inner courtyard of the Arlaten Museum.

MUSEON ARLATEN

The Provencal poet, Frédéric Mistral used to call this museum his last, great poem: he created it with the funds he received for the Nobel prize for Literature in 1904, dedicating it to the arts and local traditions of his land. The impressive Hôtel de Laval-Castellane, in 16th century style, was chosen to house it; in the courtyard is a small temple exedra which once had twelve niches where the main Roman gods were placed.

The museum has been continuously enlarged and added to since its foundation, today its 33 rooms contain a rich and picturesque documentation of the costumes, the traditions and the local history of the area thus passing on to man's collective memory the facts of daily life that are otherwise destined to disappear hardly leaving a trace of themselves. If the festival of "La Tarasque", held in Tarascon

The characteristic dragon made of canvas and papier-mâche, known as the "Tarasque".

Reconstruction of the bedroom of a newly deliverd mother receiving the visits of her friends.

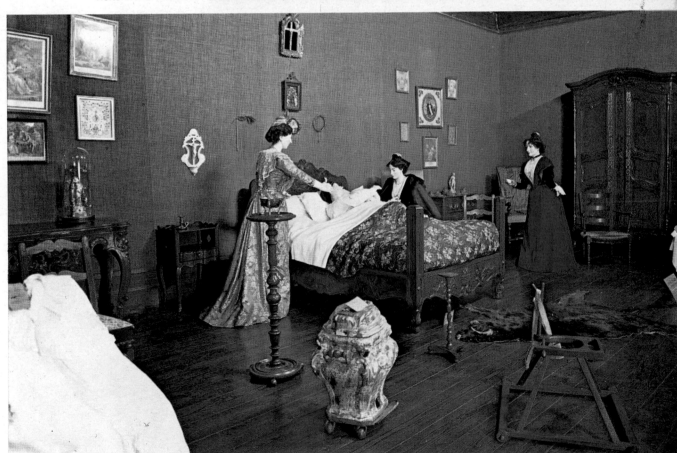

44

on the last Sunday of June, is now only for the tourists, in the museum one can follow the history of this ancient tradition that dates back to 1469. In that year "bon roi René" decreed that a fantastic dragon made from paper maché and painted cloth should be led with festivities each year through the streets of the city as reminder of the old medieval legend that a fierce beast which terrorized the area, the "Tarasque", was overcome and led on a lead like a tame little dog by St. Martha, who landed in the Camargue from far off Palestine. Among the things of most interest in the Museon Arlaten are several house interiors, accurately reconstructed in the furniture and fittings, there is a large kitchen of a house in the Camargue which emanates a sense of rustic and welcoming solidarity, and also the middle class city decor of a room where a woman with a new child is visited by her friends. The fascinating costumes that the women of Arles used to wear regularly until the beginning of the century can now only be seen on the models of the museum during some of the folk festivals. These women enchanted Van Gogh during his stay in Provence, he wrote, "J'ai vu ici des figures certes aussi belles que des Goya et des Vélasquez. Elles savent vous ficher une note rose dans un costume noir, ou bien confectionner un habillement blanc, jaune, où il n'y a rien à changer au point de vue artistique".

RÉATTU MUSEUM

The painting and applied arts collections of this museum are laid out in a monumental palace facing into the Rhone that was originally the headquarters of the Grand Prior of the knights of Malta.

The building's powerful architecture, begun in the 14th century but completed only two centuries later, reflects the warrior-like nature of the Order that it housed. The walls are of sturdy hewn blocks crowned by a high battlement beneath which waterspouts carved in the shape of lions, dragons and other threatening creatures project. When the Order of Malta was suppressed by the Revolution all its goods were auctioned and the palace was bought by the painter Jacques Réattu who lived and worked there until his death in

The inner courtyard of the Réattu Museum.

At lower left and on facing page, the characteristic gargoyles in the shape of animals.

Antoine Raspal (1738-1811) - The painter and his family.

1833. The painter's daughter then inherited it and she donated the palace to the city of Arles, in 1867.

The nucleus of the museum is the collection of paintings by Réattu, an artist of some importance in the sphere of French neo-Classical painting, and a series of canvases by his father, M. De Barrême, and his uncle Antoine Raspal, both painters from Arles. There are also collections of furniture, furnishings and cloth from different periods in the austere rooms of the Palace. Particularly worth noting is the series of Flemish Renaissance tapestries depicting *the Seven Wonders of the World*.

The Modern Art section of the museum includes paintings by Gauguin, Utrillo, Matisse and sculptures by Zadkine and Richier. Recently a donation of 57 drawings by Picasso, all from the last years of the great artist's activity, enriched the collection.

Jacques Réattu (1760-1833) -sinopite and canvas representing the Death of Alcibiades.

*François de Herain - The aged
Madelon.*

*Jacques Réattu (1760-1833) - Jacob's
vision.*

External view of the Baths of Constantine.

A partial view of the interior of the Baths. ▶

BATHS OF CONSTANTINE

A city as important and rich as Arles was during the last years of the Roman Empire could allow itself more than one Bath. There is one to the south of the forum on the site now occupied by the Place de la Republique and another to the north, known as the Palais de la Trouille. Only a few remains of the southern baths were uncovered during excavations and they do not create a clear idea of their original appearance.

On the other hand the Palais de la Trouille is an imposing building that is locally held to be the remains of a palace of Constantine. Though it cannot be proved the baths could have in fact been linked to an imperial residence, given that Constantine was especially fond of Arles and stayed there on several occasions. The vast dimensions (98 metres long by 45 wide) made it the biggest bathing establishment in the whole of Gallia Narbonese. The Baths of Constantine built around the same period (the beginning of the 4th century) at Treviri, an important city in the northern provinces of the Empire, must have had a similar lay out. The whole complex was carried out in rough hewn blocks of stone alternating with rows of bricks; today the walls of the "tepidarium" and the semi-circular apse that enclosed the "calidarium" remain standing. The latter gave rise to the name, the "Palais de la Trouille", from the Latin "trullus", an expression that describes a circular construction covered by a vault.

BOULEVARD DES LICES

The fascination of Arles does not only lie in its monuments and valuable artistic remains of a past age but of itself it is gay and at the same time pervaded by a sublte southern langour: the city invites the visitor to dally beneath the plane trees of the boulevards or in one of the many cafes facing the side-walks bathed by sun. The Boulevard des Lices follows the line of the ancient wall, on the limits of the ancient city, it is the liveliest of the city's avenues particularly on a Saturday morning when a pretty and bustling market brings together the people from the nearby Camargue and the Crau. On the first day of May the annual festival of the Guardians of the Camargue is held here, organized by the "Ancient Confraternity of the Gardian de St. Jorge", whose foundation dates from 1512. The Guardians, mounted on their steeds, crowd the boulevard and form themselves into a procession to make a circle of the city and finally receive the blessing in front of the small Gothic church of Nôtre-Dame-La-Major.

At the beginning of the Boulevard des Lices, not far from the remains of the old medieval walls and the cylindrical mass of the Tour des Morgues the public gardens offer a shady maze of avenues, recently a sculpted slab was placed here in memory of Vincent van Gogh who spent two tormented years here, though they were fruitful for his artistic production.

Two characteristic streets of Arles and, at right, two of its famous boulevards.

FOUNTAIN PICHOT

Another memorial monument, dedicated to the writer from Arles, Amadieu Pichot, is the large fountain at the meeting point of the roads of the old town centre. It was inaugurated in 1887 and is decorated with a large coloured medallion with an allegory of Poetry, the work of the local artist Paul Balze. Amadieu Pichot, a man of letters, was born in Arles on the 3rd November 1795. As a very young man he went to Paris and studied at the College of Juilly where he graduated in medicine in 1817. He was a great lover of English literature and founded the *Revue Britannique*, he also collected all the poetry inspired by the beauty of his native city into a book entitled *l'Arlesienne*.

HOPITAL VAN GOGH

It was perhaps on the advice of Toulouse-Lautrec that, in February of 1888, Vincent van Gogh decided to go to the South of France, the lights and transfiguring colours of which were to seduce the hypersensitive spirit of the great Dutch painter.
Here at Arles (where he was to remain until the end of May of the following year, before his voluntary commitment to the psychiatric hospital of Saint-

The colorful Amadieu Pichot fountain.

The entrance to the Hôtel Dieu, also known as the Hôpital van Gogh.

◀ *Open-air tables line the shady sidewalks along the boulevards.*

◀ *The massive Tour de Morgues.*

Rémy), van Gogh gave life to an incredible number of paintings and drawings. He never allowed himself to be influenced by the city's famous roman ruins nor by its most renowned artistic monuments, always preferring to paint the shaded avenues of the Alyscamps, the lazy course of the Rhone, the smoke-filled interior of a café. Frome here he was to write to his brother Théodore, nicknamed 'Théo', four years his younger: "With red and green I have tried to express the terrible human passions". It was at Arles, in fact, that the frightful madness exploded which was to lead him to suicide in July of 1890, and which reached a climax on the night of Christmas Eve when, after having attacked his friend Gauguin, van Gogh cut off his left ear with a troke of the razor.

At Arles, van Gogh soon came to know the Hôtel Dieu, the city hospital where he was confined several times for his recurrent crises; there is a beautiful canvas representing the inner courtyard, painted in April of 1889, hanging today at Winterthur, in the Sammlung Oskar Reinhart 'am Römerholz'. In the refreshing shade of the Public Gardens (formerly called the Winter Gardens), the people of Arles have erected a stele in eternal commemoration of the great painter who spent two years of his tormented existence here. "I risk my life for my work, and my reason has beeen almost destroyed by it". These words appear in a letter found on his body after Vincent van Gogh shot himself in the heart on July 29, 1890.

The plaque commemorating Vincent van Gogh, dedicated in 1969.

A view of the Public Gardens.

Overall view of the avenue of the Alyscamps.

LES ALYSCAMPS

If the arrival of the pagan invaders meant that Roman Arles ceased to exist, Christian Arles became stronger as a great religious centre throughout the Middle Ages and from this period two important monuments remain: the church of St. Trophime and the famous avenue of Les Alyscamps. The huge cemetery, whose name is a corruption of Champs Elysées, originated in a still pagan age when the local notables of the area would place their marble sarcophagi along the Via Aurelia, at the entrance of the city. From the 4th century

the place became a Christian necropolis and grew considerably throughout the Middle Ages; it was believed to have been been blessed both by St. Trophime and by Christ in person who left a trace of his appearance by the imprint of a knee on the rocky ground. Not only the inhabitants of the region but also famous people, pilgrims and foreigners wished to be buried here, and there is mention of a religious fraternity who had the task of collecting the remains of the dead of local families along the banks of the Rhone which had been enclosed in wooden coffins and entrusted to the great river to bring them to the Elysian fields

of Arles. The fame which this place, consecrated to Christian piety, enjoyed is shown by Dante himself who mentions it in Canto IX of the Inferno, while in Ariosto's Orlando Furioso the great battle between Orlando and the Saracens is set here, which goes back to an older medieval tradition according to which the brave Paladin killed at Roncivalle was buriend in Les Alyscamps.

With the passage of time the place was incredibly enriched with sarcophagi, marbles and funereal sculpture and with 19 churches or chapels. When in the 15th century the Alyscamps began to decline and was aban-

Above, a tombstone and a commemorative chapel.

Below at left, the arch of the ancient church of St. Césaire.

On the facing page, a view of the avenue and the sarcophagi with the church of St. Honorat in the background.

doned its valuable store of sculpture was continuously pillaged, often by the local authorities themselves who had no scruples about offering famous personalities the finest saracophagi or statues from Les Alyscamps. The situation was such that even Charles X, the King of France, with the intention of creating a rich collection of these tombs, loaded so many into a boat to transport them that it sank in the Rhone. Only in the last century was it realized that it was necessary to save what remained of the ancient inheritance of Les Alyscamps: there was little to compare with

Three views of the church of St. Honorat in the Alyscamps.

the treasures of sculpture that had already been dispersed but despite this the collection of sarcophagi now in the Museum of Christian Art in Arles, where the surviving works are gathered together, still have an almost equal importance with that in the Vatican Museum in Rome.

Today Alyscamps is a wide tree-lined avenue lined by rows of massive stone sarcophagi; however much it may be changed and impoverished it still preserves a deep sense of atmosphere, the same which inspired the four paintings by Van Gogh made here in the autumn of 1888.

INDEX